# BRAVE THE BIOME
# RAINFOREST
# [ SURVIVAL GUIDE ]

[ HEATHER C. HUDAK ]

CRABTREE
PUBLISHING COMPANY
WWW.CRABTREEBOOKS.COM

# BRAVE THE BIOME

**Author:** Heather C. Hudak

**Editors:** Sarah Eason, Jennifer Sanderson, and Ellen Rodger

**Proofreader and indexer:** Tracey Kelly

**Proofreader:** Petrice Custance

**Editorial director:** Kathy Middleton

**Design:** Jessica Moon

**Cover design:** Tammy McGarr

**Photo research:** Rachel Blount

**Production coordinator and Prepress technician:** Tammy McGarr

**Print coordinator:** Katherine Berti

**Consultant:** David Hawksett

Produced for Crabtree Publishing by Calcium

**Photo Credits:**
t=Top, c=Center, b=Bottom, l= Left, r=Right

**Inside:** Jessica Moon: p. 29t; Shutterstock: AF-Photography: p. 22b; Al&#39;fred: pp. 30–31; Alexander P: p. 23b; Ophat Angworakun: p. 4; Apiguide: pp. 4–5, 32; Shamil Ashraf: p. 17t; DarwelShots: pp. 18–19; Adalbert Dragon: p. 6t; Ervin-Edward: pp. 12–13; Ficus777: p. 7b; Fijalka: pp. 14–15; Fotos593: pp. 11t, 16–17; Heather Goodman: p. 21r; Rene Holtslag: pp. 8–9; Juhku: p. 12t; Roman Khomlyak: pp. 22–23; Mariia Korneeva: pp. 8–9b; Yevgen Kravchenko: p. 25b; Lineartestpilot: p. 19b; James Aloysius Mahan V: p. 23t; Maridav: p. 26l; MaXo Family: p. 19t; Milhad: p. 11b; Natspace: p. 16b; Navigator-tour: pp. 20–21; Carlos Neto: p. 18l; Anastasia Nio: p. 19br; Ntonkova: pp. 24–25; Elena Odareeva: p. 17b; Grigorii Pisotsckii: p. 24b; Richardmak: p. 6; Ooriya Ron: p. 14l; Rsfatt: p. 29b; Dmitry Shanchuk: p. 13b; Vova Shevchuk: pp. 10–11; Soft light: pp. 28–29; Stella E: p. 6b; Mr. Tempter: pp. 24–25t; Worldclassphoto: pp. 26–27; Worldswildlifewonders: p. 5t.

**Cover:** All images from Shutterstock

## Library and Archives Canada Cataloguing in Publication

Title: Rainforest survival guide / Heather C. Hudak.
Names: Hudak, Heather C., 1975- author.
Description: Series statement: Brave the biome | Includes index.
Identifiers: Canadiana (print) 20200286382 |
  Canadiana (ebook) 20200286404 |
  ISBN 9780778781363 (softcover) |
  ISBN 9780778781301 (hardcover) |
  ISBN 9781427125767 (HTML)
Subjects: LCSH: Survival—Juvenile literature. |
  LCSH: Rain forests—Juvenile literature.
Classification: LCC GV200.5 .H83 2021 | DDC j613.6/909152—dc23

## Library of Congress Cataloging-in-Publication Data

Names: Hudak, Heather C., 1975- author.
Title: Rainforest survival guide / Heather C. Hudak.
Description: New York : Crabtree Publishing Company, [2021] |
  Series: Brave the biome | Includes index.
Identifiers: LCCN 2020029954 (print) | LCCN 2020029955 (ebook) |
  ISBN 9780778781301 (hardcover) |
  ISBN 9780778781363 (paperback) |
  ISBN 9781427125767 (ebook)
Subjects: LCSH: Jungle survival--Juvenile literature. | Rain forests--Juvenile literature. | Wilderness survival--Juvenile literature.
Classification: LCC GV200.5 .H834 2021 (print) |
  LCC GV200.5 (ebook) | DDC 613.6/909152--dc23
LC record available at https://lccn.loc.gov/2020029954
LC ebook record available at https://lccn.loc.gov/2020029955

## Crabtree Publishing Company

www.crabtreebooks.com    1-800-387-7650

Printed in the U.S.A./092020/CG20200810

**Published in Canada**
**Crabtree Publishing**
616 Welland Ave.
St. Catharines, Ontario
L2M 5V6

**Published in the United States**
**Crabtree Publishing**
347 Fifth Ave.
Suite 1402-145
New York, NY 10016

**Published in the United Kingdom**
**Crabtree Publishing**
Maritime House
Basin Road North, Hove
BN41 1WR

**Published in Australia**
**Crabtree Publishing**
3 Charles Street
Coburg North
VIC, 3058

# CONTENTS

Rain forests are one of the most difficult **biomes** for humans to survive in. They are home to **predators** and poisonous plants. Heavy rainfall can lead to mudslides and floods. Fallen trees and thick **undergrowth** on the forest floor makes it difficult to travel by foot and can lead to serious injuries. Understanding the dangers of rainforest **environments** and having keen survival skills can make the difference between life and death.

## CATCHING THE RAIN

Rain forests get plenty of rain every day. This makes it easier for people lost in the rain forest to find water to drink. Tall trees block the Sun's rays from reaching the undergrowth, so plants that live in the rainforest **understory** and on the forest floor grow big leaves to absorb more sunlight. Hikers can use these large leaves as a bowl to collect rainwater and dew to drink. They can place a leaf on the edge of a container, and the water that pools in the leaf will then flow into the container.

Thinking about any problems explorers may face in a rain forest, and the survival skills they might need, can help them stay alive.

## MOVING AROUND

Tropical rain forests, such as the Amazon Basin in South America, grow near the equator in places that have hot, **humid** climates. Temperate rain forests grow in places where it is cooler, such as the Pacific coast of Canada and the United States. The animals that are found there have **adapted** to live among the thousands of tree species. Spider monkeys use their long, strong tail and limbs to swing from branches. Humans find it much harder to move around. Some rainforest explorers use hatchets or large knives called machetes to cut through thick **vegetation**.

spider ········· monkey

## LOOK FOR ...

Look for the "How to Survive" and "Be Prepared" features in this book. These list many of the techniques that people have used to survive in rain forests.

One of the best ways to stay safe in the rain forest is to travel in a group with an experienced guide. Groups should let someone outside of the group know their route and when they expect to return. That way, if they do not return at the planned time, that person can call for help. It is easy to get lost in the forest, so people should never stray from their group or the trail.

## WILDLIFE DANGERS

Most animals run away in fear at the sight of a human. If explorers do see a wild animal in the rain forest, such as a jaguar, the most important thing for them to do is to keep calm. Running away can trigger a predator's **chase instinct**. If an animal approaches, making loud sounds can help scare it away. Hiding behind trees can also put a distance between the person and the animal.

jaguar

Explorers should map their route before going into the rain forest. They can mark any rivers and mountains that may make their hike more difficult.

## WHAT TO WEAR

When hiking through the rain forest, people need to cover as much skin as possible. Long sleeves, long pants, and head and neck coverings help protect against mosquitoes and other insect bites. Lightweight clothing is breathable and helps keep people cool. Daily rain and fog make everything moist, so it is a good idea for travelers to pack a raincoat or water-resistant poncho to layer over their clothes. Sturdy waterproof shoes or rubber jungle boots keep people's feet dry and protect against bites and stings.

## HOW TO KEEP FEET DRY

It is essential for people to keep their feet dry in the rain forest. Wet feet can lead to **fungus** and other problems. Wrapping feet in a plastic bag before putting on non-waterproof shoes helps keep feet dry.

Protective footwear, such as hiking boots, is important for traveling in the rain forest.

# PLANE CRASH SURVIVOR:
## JULIANE KOEPCKE

In 1971, 17-year-old Juliane Koepcke was stranded in the tropical Amazon rain forest when the plane she was traveling on crashed. Every passenger on board died—except Juliane. The teenager then spent 10 days fighting for her life in the rain forest.

## DISASTER STRIKES

Juliane and her mother boarded a flight to Pucallpa, Peru. About one hour into their flight, lightning struck the plane, and it broke apart. Juliane fell through the sky, strapped to her seat. When she awoke, she was in the rain forest. She had cuts on her legs and a broken collarbone, but she had a strong instinct to survive. She had spent two years living at an Amazon rainforest **research station** with her parents, so she knew the dangers of the rain forest and how to avoid them. Julianne found a bag of candies in the plane wreckage. She took them with her in case she could not find any food that was safe to eat.

## SURVIVAL INSTINCTS

When Juliane came across a stream, she recalled her father saying she should walk along the water if she was ever lost in the rain forest. She knew that a small stream would lead to a bigger one, and that people often live by the water. Juliane walked and swam along the stream. After nine days, she could barely walk, so she drifted along the river. Finally, she spotted a boat and a nearby path. She followed the path to a hut and rested there for the night.

## RESCUED AT LAST

Juliane woke up to the sound of voices. Three men who lived in the hut had come home. They treated her wounds and fed her before taking her to a nearby town the next day. Juliane was reunited with her father the day after her rescue. She also helped the local authorities locate the plane wreckage. To this day, no one knows how she survived the crash. But it was thanks to her knowledge of basic survival skills that she made it through the next 10 days.

Young people are **resilient**, and many studies have proven that if they are educated in survival skills, they have a good chance of making it through disasters.

If lost or stranded in a rain forest, it is best to stay in one place until help arrives. However, it can be difficult for rescuers searching from the air to spot people through the trees. Sometimes, the only option is for explorers to try to find their own way out of the rain forest.

## LOOK FOR LANDFORMS

There are few landmarks to help guide people out of a rain forest. The thick vegetation makes it hard to see rivers, lakes, mountains, valleys, and other landforms that people usually use as markers along their route. It is best for explorers to find higher ground where they can observe the area. From there, they can look for a clearing where rescuers might be able to see them better. If there is no obvious way to travel, walking in one direction would be a better option.

Following the route of water, such as a stream or a river, is a good skill to use in a survival situation. Running water often leads to settlements and people.

## BE ON THE LOOKOUT

It is important for those who are lost to travel slowly, so they can save energy. It helps to look for gaps in the trees that can be cut through to get out quicker. They may even find an animal trail that leads to a source of water. Animals, from small reptiles to large cats, can be difficult to see because of their camouflage, but there are signs to look for. These include scat, or poop, and paw prints.

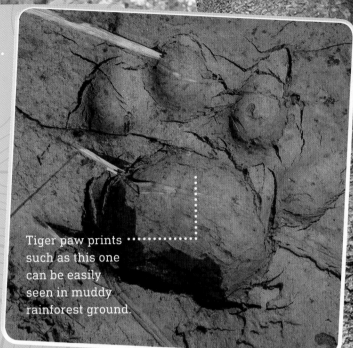

Tiger paw prints such as this one can be easily seen in muddy rainforest ground.

## BE PREPARED

The rainforest ground is most often wet and slippery. Explorers need to step carefully as they walk, so they do not lose their balance. They could twist an ankle or break a leg. Never walk barefoot through the forest. Bug bites are also a problem, and **parasites** can burrow into the skin. It is important for people to keep their eyes to the ground to avoid biting insects, such as bullet ants.

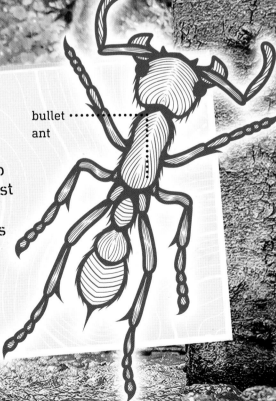

bullet ant

**M**any rainforest plants have leaves with serrated, or jagged, edges or spiky thorns that tear or scratch the skin. Others are covered with hairs that sting and prick. An explorer may walk away with only a cut or scrape, but in a rain forest, any open wound could lead to an infection.

## PAINFUL PLANTS

Sometimes, grabbing onto trees or vines is the only way to climb up a steep hill or down into a valley, but this can be dangerous. For example, the wait-a-while vine hangs from the **canopy** to the floor in Australia's tropical rain forests. It is covered in hooked spines that latch onto people and rip their skin. Rattan is a type of vine that grows in Asia. Its thorny stem can slash through a human hand. People should try to stay on trails that have been cleared of vegetation wherever they can.

rattan plant

Touching plants and leaves can be dangerous. This is because some leaves, such as those of fan palms, end in sharp, thorny points. Rainforest cacti have spines that can puncture flesh.

## TOXIC TOUCH

Many plants are covered in substances that can damage or irritate the skin. Some cause itching and swelling. Others burn or leave rashes and blisters. Wearing a lightweight pair of gloves and covering exposed skin can help prevent contact. After coming into contact with plants, it is important to wash hands thoroughly. If there are any thorns or spikes on a person's skin, pulling them out gently and putting a bandage over the damaged area can limit infection.

## BE PREPARED

A long, straight branch or bamboo stalk makes the perfect walking stick. It can be used to keep balance and reduce slips and trips. Walking sticks can be used to clear a path through vegetation. This prevents the hands from coming into contact with plants. A stick can also be used to poke the ground for spiders, snakes, scorpions, and insects.

scorpion ·····

# THE LOST TRAIL:
## DAVID TAMOWSKI

David Tamowski had more than 10 years of experience backpacking. Still, he got lost in the temperate rain forest of New Zealand's Mount Aspiring National Park for 10 days in April, 2015. David missed important steps when planning his hike, and that made the difference between staying safe and getting stranded.

## STARTING OUT

David was flying from his home in Utah to visit his wife's family in Auckland, New Zealand. He decided to spend a few days hiking on his own before meeting up with them. Before starting his journey, David worked with locals to plan a route and mark it on a map. Soon after setting out, David realized he had forgotten to pack a beacon, a device that sends a signal and location if a backpacker gets lost. He continued on anyway.

## NO WAY OUT

The first two days went well, but after that, fog settled over the area. David could barely see the trail, but again, he kept going. By the time the fog lifted, David had lost the trail. His only way back was down a steep slope. As he started working his way down the slope, his compass fell to the ground. He checked for his map, but it was gone, too. It was morning before he made his way to the bottom of the slope. David then followed a riverbank, thinking it would lead him out of the forest, but it led to a waterfall. David was trapped in all directions by cliffs and waterfalls. He made an "X" out of rocks as a signal, but still no one came.

## GETTING OUT

David was running out of food and losing hope. Finally, he found a large meadow. He knew that rescuers would have a better view of him from above. Soon after, he heard a helicopter and raced to make a fire with branches. But the helicopter did not see him. The next day, another helicopter passed over. David waved his arms and shouted until he caught the pilot's attention. The pilot was a hunter who saw David by accident. David was nowhere near his planned route where rescuers had been searching for him, so he was lucky to be rescued.

*Many travelers are drawn to Mount Aspiring National Park because of its beautiful mountains, river valleys, and stunning lakes.*

One of the first things explorers should do when lost in the rain forest is look for a source of water. Not only do they need water to survive, but there is also a higher chance of finding help near a body of water. Water always flows downhill, so people can look for a slope or low-lying areas and go in that direction. It will eventually lead to a source of water that they can follow. Another way to find water is to look for animal tracks. Often, they will lead to a watering hole, where animals gather to drink.

## DIRTY WATER

Not all rainforest water is safe to drink. Muddy pools that do not flow or move can contain **bacteria**. Even crystal clear standing waters could be filled with pollutants such as animal waste. Fast-moving water, such as a river, is best. Layers of soil, sand, rock, and other natural materials help **filter** the water as it moves, so it is less likely to be **contaminated**.

## HOW TO GET WATER FROM BAMBOO

·····•···· bamboo

Green bamboo stalks may contain water that is clear, odorless, and safe to drink. Bending the bamboo stalk toward the ground will cause the water to flow to one end. Cutting off the top will let the water drip out.

## DIG FOR WATER

Sometimes, water can be found by digging a hole in a muddy area. The hole may fill with water, which can be soaked up in a cloth. Another option is to build a **solar water still** by digging a deep, wide hole in a moist, sunny spot and covering the hole with a plastic bag. A container should be put inside the hole before covering it. **Condensation** will form on the plastic and drip into the container below.

underground water

Staying well hydrated at all times in the rain forest is important. High temperatures and sweating lead to water loss and dehydration.

**F**ruit, fish, nuts, and insects are just a few of the foods that are easy to find in the rain forest. But not all are edible, and some are deadly. Before heading into the forest, it is a good idea to learn about the plants and animals that are safe to eat. It is also useful to carry a field guide to help identify unsafe foods in the forest.

## LOOK FOR FAMILIAR FRUITS

Mangoes, yams, bananas, papayas, avocados, figs, peanuts, cashews, cucumbers, pineapples, and coconuts are common in many rain forests. They can be plucked straight from the plants or gathered off the ground. Many species of berries and mushrooms are toxic. If a person is unsure of a plant, it is best not to eat it. It is also important to take only what can be eaten at the moment. Food rots quickly in the heat, and the odor can attract unwanted insects and animals.

The banana is an important food found in rain forests. About two-thirds of the world's plant species grow in rain forests.

## EATING INSECTS

Worms, grasshoppers, crickets, termites, ants, and grubs are excellent sources of protein. However, many insects are poisonous. Bright colors and strong smells are often signs of danger. Insects that sting, bite, or are covered in hairs can also be harmful. It is a important to cook insects before eating them. This can help destroy any poisons or parasites they may carry.

Bamboo worms are high in protein and fiber. They are a popular food in parts of Asia.

## HOW TO CATCH FISH

Fish are plentiful in forest rivers. A fishing spear can be made by sharpening the end of a long, straight branch or bamboo stalk to a point. When a fish swims nearby, both hands can be used to jab it with the spear.

# BRUISED, BURNED, AND BITTEN:
## SHANNON FRASER

In the fall of 2014, Shannon Fraser was at a swimming hole near her home in Australia, when she had a fight with her boyfriend and ran into the tropical rain forest. Shannon decided to rest but fell asleep. When she awoke, she was confused, lost, and alone. She spent 17 days in the rain forest before finding her way out.

## OFF THE BEATEN PATH

When Shannon could not find the trail, she panicked and began to wander deeper into the forest instead of tracking the river back to the swimming hole. She spent a whole day climbing through stinging bushes and wait-a-while vines to reach the top of the tallest mountain in Queensland, Mount Bartle Frere. Rescuers never looked in the area because they did not think that Shannon could move through that part of the forest without a large knife to chop a trail through the plants. Helicopters could not spot Shannon through the thick trees.

## NAKED AND AFRAID

Shannon was wearing leggings, a shirt, and flip flops when she went missing. The trees ripped off most of her clothes, so she had little protection from the Sun. Her entire body was badly burned. After 12 days in the forest, Shannon tried following the river. She knew there could be dangerous animals in the water, such as crocodiles, but got in anyway. She spent an entire day swimming downstream with no luck. Despairing, she spent the next three days huddled on a rock. Starving and covered in infected wounds, Shannon was sure she would die there.

## OUT OF THE WOODS

On day 16, Shannon decided to try one last time to find help. She walked all day. Finally, she spotted a pink ribbon on a tree. She knew it meant that rescuers had looked for her there. She saw more markers on the trees and followed them to a path. When she eventually stumbled out of the rain forest, she was **dehydrated** and covered in insect bites. A farmer had heard Shannon's screams and realized who she was. He helped her out of the woods. She had faced unimaginable dangers but she survived against the odds by eating insects and small fish, and never giving up.

*No one should ever enter the rain forest unless they are wearing proper clothing, including long-sleeved tops and pants. Bare skin can be easily cut and torn or bitten by insects in the forest.*

Aside from food and water, shelter is a top **priority** for anyone lost in the rain forest. Shelter provides protection from the wind, humidity, and rain. It also offers a safe place to rest and hide from predators.

## PREMADE SHELTER

Some trees have huge roots that can be used for shelter. A roof can be formed by placing branches, palm leaves, or a plastic bag on top of the roots. Hollowed-out trees, old animal dens, and empty caves can be used for shelter if they are not being used by any animals. Animals could become aggressive if they find someone inside their home.

Being able to make a fire is one of the most important survival skills a person can have. Fire can be used for light and warmth and to cook food and boil water. The smoke helps keep insects away. Fire can also be used to scare animals away or signal for help from rescuers.

## BUILD A LEAN-TO

It is a good idea for travelers to carry plastic sheeting and rope when hiking in the rain forest. They can tie the rope between two trees and hang the plastic on top to make a tent. If no rope or plastic is available, a shelter can be built using materials on the forest floor, such as branches and large, wide leaves. A lean-to is the easiest type of shelter to build in the rain forest. It is a simple structure made by leaning a branch against a tree and covering it with other branches and leaves. It is best to build a shelter away from cliff edges, fast-moving waters, dead trees that can fall at any time, and other **hazards**. The ground should be checked carefully for insect nests and animal burrows.

lean-to shelter ·········

## HOW TO START A FIRE

To start a fire in a rain forest, cut a notch near one end of a small, dry branch. Put a second branch inside the notch, and roll it quickly back and forth between the hands. This rolling movement creates **friction**, which makes the wood very hot and smoky.

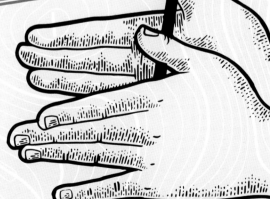

**R**ain forests are home to some of the largest rivers in the world, such as the Nile River in Africa and the Mekong River in China. Many streams, creeks, and **tributaries** feed into these large rivers. As a result, one of the quickest ways out of a rain forest is to follow running water to a river, then travel along it.

## WATCH OUT FOR WILDLIFE

Swimming down a river is faster than trying to walk through a forest. However, many dangerous animals lurk beneath the water. Caimans, a type of alligator, are fast swimmers and have strong jaws for crushing their **prey**. In South America, massive snakes called anacondas hide in the water waiting for prey to come near. Then, they grab it and **constrict** it. Electric eels are known for their powerful shock, while piranhas have razor-sharp teeth and attack in groups.

piranha

## DO NOT GET CARRIED AWAY

One way to keep safe in rainforest waters is to use a raft. A raft can be made by tying long tree branches together with vines and tree bark. Branches and rocks hidden under the water can make for a rough ride on the raft, and strong **currents** can sweep the raft off course. This is a big concern if there are waterfalls or cliffs nearby that the raft could go over. In such cases, it is best for explorers to come ashore and carry their raft by land until it is safe to go back in the water.

When swimming in a rainforest river, people can use equipment such as backpacks to help keep them afloat.

## HOW TO BUILD A BAMBOO RAFT

Bamboo is one of the best materials to use to make a raft. The stalks are hollow and float well. Bamboo stalks that are about 10-feet (3 m) long should be laid side by side on the ground. A hole needs to be made at both ends and in the center of each stalk. Vines can then be threaded through the holes to lash the stalks together. Attaching cross poles to the bottom of the raft will make it sturdier.

raft

# FACING A JAGUAR:
## YOSSI GHINSBERG

Yossi Ghinsberg had just completed his military service with the Israeli Navy when he set out to explore the world. He never imagined that he would find himself lost in the Amazon rain forest for three weeks.

## RAINFOREST ADVENTURERS

In 1981, Yossi was backpacking through Bolivia when he met up with three other men who were also looking for an adventure. One of the men was an experienced rainforest explorer. He told the others of the great fun they could have searching for a hidden tribe and lost riches in the Amazon rain forest. Locals warned the men of the dangers they would face, but the group decided to go ahead with their trip.

*The wild landscape of places such as the rain forest is appealing to young travelers, but these places are full of many dangers.*

## TROUBLE ON THE WATER

During their trip, the four men were not getting along well, and they decided to split up. One of the men wanted to build a raft to travel by, and Yossi joined him. However, disaster struck when they lost control and Yossi was thrown over a waterfall. He survived the fall only to realize he was alone. Days passed with no sign of anyone else. Yossi began to walk in what he thought was the direction of the nearest town.

## THE WILL TO SURVIVE

Yossi ate raw eggs that he found in nests and moldy fruit that fell from the trees. He had to defend himself from giant red ants, a wild boar, and snakes. He even made a flamethrower from insect repellent to ward off a jaguar. Yossi started to lose hope after he nearly drowned in a flood. His food had run out, and he had no energy to keep going. Parasites had burrowed beneath his skin. His feet were so sore he could barely move. Yossi shook fire ants from a tree onto his head to distract himself from the pain.

## BARELY ALIVE

Then, one day, the man Yossi had been traveling with arrived in a boat to rescue him. The man had made his way to a nearby village, and the locals offered to help him find Yossi. They had given up hope of finding Yossi alive. They were looking for a place to turn their boat around when they spotted Yossi. He had collapsed and was close to starvation. The other two men that Yossi had been traveling with were never seen again.

**K**eeping positive and determined to survive is an important part of survival. People lost in the rain forest can think about family and friends and happy memories of home to keep them going when life gets tough. Although survival in a rain forest is never easy, people who know basic survival skills have a better chance of making it out of the rain forest alive. There are steps rainforest explorers can take to keep safe and help rescuers find them.

## STOP FOR A MINUTE

People lost in the forest can use the STOP method to help them survive. The "S" in STOP stands for "staying calm." It is much easier to make good choices when a person does not panic. The "T" is for "thinking about the situation for a moment before taking action." The "O" means to "observe the area and get **oriented**." Looking for broken branches or other clues about the original direction of travel can help people find their way back to civilization. Finally, the "P" in STOP is for "planning." It is never a good idea to walk aimlessly through a forest. It is always best to have a plan before moving in any direction. Leaving a note at the starting point will let potential rescuers know the plan.

Panicking is one of the worst things to do if a person is lost. Using the STOP method can help calm the mind, allowing a person to pause and think through their situation.

# HOW TO SIGNAL FOR HELP

Distress signals are a way to help rescuers find people who are lost in a forest. Blowing a whistle is one way to send out a distress signal. If there is no whistle, one can be made by cutting a hole in a hollow piece of wood. Bright lights can be seen from miles away, so explorers can use a mirror to **reflect** the Sun's light. When lost in a thick forest, rescue safety experts suggest looking for a clearing and using forest materials, such as rocks or branches, to spell out a short message. **SOS**, HELP, or an X work well. The goal is to attract attention. If the letters are big enough, rescuers will be able to see them from above. If there is no other option, smoke signals can be used. A big, smoky fire can be seen from a distance or above the trees. Burning green leaves creates a lot of smoke.

## LOOK FOR LOCALS

Many **Indigenous peoples** have lived in rain forests for thousands of years. Traditionally, they relied on the rain forest for food, shelter, medicine, and everything else they needed to survive. Few indigenous groups rely solely on traditional ways of living today. Still, they know the rainforest environment better than anyone else.

# GLOSSARY

**adapted** Developed skills or physical features over time to help animals live in a certain biome

**bacteria** Single-celled organisms that are invisible to the human eye

**biomes** Large areas where plants and animals naturally live. A biome is also recognized by other features, such as how much water it has and what its weather is like.

**canopy** The top layer of the rain forest

**chase instinct** An animal's natural reaction to chase prey

**condensation** The process of water vapor in the air cooling and turning into water

**constrict** Squeeze tighter

**contaminated** Filled with substances that make something impure

**currents** The flow of air or water in a certain direction

**dehydrated** Describes someone suffering from extreme loss of water from the body

**environments** Surroundings

**filter** Remove unwanted particles

**friction** The rubbing of an object over another object

**fungus** Living organisms that are neither plants nor animals and that feed on other organisms by causing them to rot

**hazards** Dangerous things

**humid** Having a large amount of water or moisture in the air

**Indigenous peoples** The original inhabitants of a land

**oriented** Positioned in a certain direction

**parasites** Organisms that live and feed on other animals

**predators** Animals that hunt and eat other animals

**prey** Animals that are chased and eaten by other animals

**resilient** Able to recover quickly from a difficult situation

SOS A universal rescue signal that stands for Save Our Souls

**priority** The order in which something comes or is done

**reflect** Bounce back to its source

**research station** A place where scientists work and live while they study the surroundings

**solar water still** A device that uses heat from the Sun's rays to produce clean drinking water

**tributaries** Rivers or streams that feed into a larger river or lake

**undergrowth** Small plants that grow on the forest floor

**understory** The layer of plants and trees beneath the canopy

**vegetation** Plants and trees

## LEARNING MORE

Find out more about rain forests and how to survive them.

Bailey, Gerry. *Tangled in the Rainforest*. Crabtree Publishing Company, 2014.

Grylls, Bear. *The Jungle Challenge* (A Bear Grylls Adventure). Bear Grylls Publishing, 2017.

Hyde, Natalie. *Amazon Rainforest Research Journal*. Crabtree Publishing Company, 2018.

Long, Denise. *Survival Kid: A Practical Guide to Wilderness Survival*. Chicago Review Press, 2011.

## WEBSITES

Find out more about how to survive in the rain forest at:
**https://adventure.howstuffworks.com/survival/wilderness/jungle-survival.htm**

Get to know the Indigenous peoples who live in the rain forest at:
**https://rainforests.mongabay.com/amazon/amazon_people.html**

Learn more about the dangerous animals that live in the rain forest at:
**https://sciencing.com/deadly-animals-live-rainforest-8120242.html**

Discover fun facts about rain forests at:
**www.rainforest-alliance.org/pictures/9-rainforest-facts-everyone-should-know**

## INDEX

## ABOUT THE AUTHOR

Heather C. Hudak has written hundreds of books for kids. When she's not writing, Heather loves to travel the world. She has been to all kinds of biomes, from deserts to mountains and everything in between. Some of Heather's favorite journeys have taken her through the lush rain forests of Asia, North America, and South America.